INNERSPACE

By the same author

Starbright
Moonbeam
Sunshine
The Inner Garden

The Art of Inner Learning

INNERSPACE

Meditations for Students of Life

MAUREEN GARTH

HarperCollins*Publishers*

Published by HarperCollins*Religious*
(ACN 005 677 805)
A member of the HarperCollins*Publishers* (Australia) Pty Ltd group
22–24 Joseph Street
North Blackburn, Victoria 3130, Australia

First published 1995
Designed by Pierluigi Vido
Cover design by Pierluigi Vido
Cover illustration by Liz Dixon
Illustrations by Liz Dixon
Typeset in Janson and Gill by HarperCollins*Publishers*, Melbourne
Printed in Australia by Griffin Paperbacks

National Library of Australia Cataloguing-in-Publication data:

Garth, Maureen.

InnerSpace: the art of inner learning: meditations for students of life.

ISBN 1 86371 591 6.

1. Meditation. 2. Meditations. I. Title. II. Title: InnerSpace.

158.12

To Eleanor

For Her Light

and Beauty

of Soul

CONTENTS

INTRODUCTION

Meditation enables a peace and serenity that we may not have experienced before to flow through our lives, our thoughts, our being. In today's frenetic lifestyle, it is important to take time out for ourselves in order to nourish the inner person. Our core self is sometimes left behind as we try to keep in step with others. We may find we are going at a pace that is wrong for us and does not support our inner needs. Meditation means taking time out for the self, sitting quietly in order to tune in to feelings of peace, harmony and well-being. We all need more peace and quiet within the self, and to feel we are strong enough spiritually to cope with whatever life gives us.

This book has been written primarily for young people, as they are needy. They have to cope with enormous stress in order to achieve and encounter many difficulties in their quest for a better life. However, people of all ages will benefit from what I have written. The meditations can be used in all aspects of life for people who want to be creative, overcome obstacles, gain a better perspective, develop creativity, become flexible and able to forgive, aim high and have abundance, and achieve in life what is rightfully theirs.

Why you should meditate

Whatever you do or learn nowadays can be stressful. Learning today is quite different from the time of your parents. It is more complex and life is more difficult than it was during their childhood and schooling.

Computers are now taught in kindergarten, there is a far wider range of subjects, and it is becoming more and more difficult to achieve, to attain the highest standards, because the competition nowadays is fierce. When you leave your place of learning, there is uncertainty about what you want to do with your life and whether the career of your choice is available.

Meditation can help you set up scenarios to achieve the goals you want in life. For instance, if there is an exam coming up, you could go into the meditative state and take yourself through the exam by seeing the examination room, the table you will use, the chair you will sit on, the pens and pencils you will write with. You could see how your hand, holding the pen, flies across the page, correctly answering each question and completing the test paper with ease.

Through meditation and visualization, you could see yourself applying for a position, feeling very positive about yourself and your abilities, and being accepted.

This sounds very simple, but it works. Whatever you feed into your mind, be it positive or negative, comes out the way you have foreseen or programmed it.

If you look at only negative aspects, then you will find that everything you are doing is colored by this negativity, and what comes through will not be what you are wanting to attain.

Too often you hear people say, "But I am no good at that" or "I am sure I will fail my exams." The very act of saying "I am no good" or "I will fail" indicates the mind accepting that these things are true for you, and therefore what follows will be like wish fulfillment. Within the heart of the person making these statements is often the wish that some other person will confirm that they can accomplish and achieve when they should be confirming it to themselves.

A positive attitude, accompanied by perseverance and a desire to succeed, will bring results that may surprise you. If you take the attitude, the perseverance, the desire to succeed, and use these in your meditative state by seeing how well you can accomplish your desire, you are setting up within yourself the ability to bring forth the very best *you* there is.

Like a tree, you have an inner strength. If your roots are firm and secure, this inner strength will flow into all areas of your life. Inner strength cannot be given to you. It is either something you acquire through meeting life's challenges, or something you have always had.

Growing, maturing, changing, means that many aspects of the self change although sometimes there are parts that get left behind, parts that we may yearn for, the small child that was. But that small child will live forever within the self. You will find that there are many selves that have lived and still continue to influence your living as you change and grow.

Meditation is not new. People have practiced meditation throughout the ages in many different cultures. It is used in churches, Buddhist temples, ashrams, mosques and synagogues, in homes, or when communing with nature in the open air. Although each of the major belief systems meditates in a different way, all come back to going within, to listening to the inner self, to becoming in tune with the self and nature. Some people like to meditate to a mantra, to a sound, to quiet music, to prayer. And others require nothing but silence.

Meditation allows a calmness and a serenity that otherwise may be lacking to enter your life. Such qualities can bring peacefulness and a sense of belonging to the Universe, of being at one with all that exists.

Meditation can make you more aware of people and their needs, more tolerant of the failings of others, and more forgiving of your own failings.

Imagination and visualization

The vast majority of people seem to take to meditation more easily if they are given a process whereby they are encouraged to visualize, to use their imagination.

Some people may think that imagining, or "daydreaming," is an unrealistic way to spend time. What they do not realize is that imagining is a form of meditation. Imagination is creative. Without imagination, there would be no books written, no paintings painted. People who create art or who are pioneers in industry, people who climb mountains, use their imagination to create thoughts, ideas and images which they then activate. They are often meditating, knowingly or unknowingly, and they bring their images together while in the meditative state.

Visualization is different to imagination. Visualization means putting thoughts and images into a more concrete form so that we can actively work on the images. By meditating in this way we create a scene or an image within ourselves upon which we can work to benefit our everyday life.

If we have a strong enough belief, what we are visualizing can be played back into real life. Our daydreaming can be constructive and not time-wasting. Our creativity can flow when we daydream. Our thoughts can wander from our present limited pattern to a more relaxed and developed way of looking at what we want in life. What we are doing is working with the mind and not limiting it by guidelines or boundaries that could be restrictive. There is no need to restrict ourselves when meditating.

I believe we can use meditation to visualize what we need in our lives, whether it be strength, love of life or people, a happier environment, better study skills, a better place of work, better health. In meditation we go to an inner part of ourselves where, by sitting quietly, the breathing slows, the heart quietens, and we learn the answers to our troubles.

Meditation means going within, listening to the inner or higher self, while visualization means using visual pictures in the meditative state to create what you need in your life.

Sometimes we do not get what we think we want, either because we have not visualized it strongly enough or because, at some deeper inner level, we know it isn't the right thing for us.

You may recall that as a small child you would drift "off" into a different world, one of your own where no one else could enter. Your concentration span would have been short, but you would have been able to concentrate intensely for brief periods of time. Perhaps you became absorbed in watching a bee pollinate a flower, or an ant carrying something as large as itself, or perhaps your mind just drifted, full of odd images. You would have been daydreaming, and that is similar to meditation.

The difference between daydreaming and meditation is that one allows the mind to wander and the other uses the mind constructively.

When we daydream, all sorts of thoughts and images pop into our minds. We can look at a flower and note the color and texture of the petal, the small ant crawling up the stem, the strength of the leaf.

When we meditate, we can see with our inner eye the flower, the petal, the ant, the leaf, but we can also go beyond that. We might feel as though we *are* the flower, the ant, the leaf, the petal. We might also feel the roots of the bush going deep into the earth, and the moisture the earth contains that nourishes those roots.

Meditation can take us far away from the surface parts of ourselves, into areas that need to be nourished. There we can reach out and grow differently in a process that will be reflected positively in our personal lives.

Our inner resources

We all need a place in which to feel secure, to feel centered, to feel connected. Often we roam the earth, figuratively speaking, seeking such things and not securing them because we are looking in the wrong places. We need to look within.

Looking without for the answers doesn't work. We keep chasing answers and, like rainbows, they keep eluding us. If we realised that our inner selves hold the key, then we would know that all we need do is to go within.

And that is what meditation does. It allows us to go within, to seek, to think, to find, to ponder. It allows our minds to be flexible, to roam, to be free.

Through meditation we can look at our goals. Sometimes we may feel non-specific about some of our goals and not able to come to grips with how to bring them into a positive context. By sitting quietly, going into our mental garden, we can often define what to do, and how to do it.

All of my meditations take place in a lovely garden. This garden is not an external garden, but one that lives inside each of us and is therefore easily accessible. It is somewhere to go that is specifically yours. When you close the gate behind you, you have entered the garden and its peaceful state. There, nothing can harm you; everyone lives together peacefully, including the animals; nothing ever dies because there is no death.

The serenity and peace that you will find within your garden will reflect back into your outer world, enabling you to feel good about yourself and your surroundings.

There is a need to call on all our resources early in life, and one of these resources could be meditation. If we learn early the discipline of meditating, we are setting up a practice that will carry us through our lives aware that it gains us knowledge and security of self.

When we work on our inner resources, we can change patterns that have been there for years. Some of these patterns may involve the conviction that we are not good enough, not bright enough, not popular enough, and that we cannot achieve. Self-esteem or self-worth may be at either end of the scale, either too low or perhaps too abrasive. If it is too abrasive, we may be over-compensating for a lack in a different area and this would need to be looked at. If it is too low, then we need to look at how to bolster our self-worth so that we feel good about the self.

All through our formative years we have done this processing on the internal level, whether we have been aware of it or not. What our parents tell us, our teachers, our friends, is formatted inside as though we are computers. What we think we are, as opposed to what others tell us, is also "wired" within.

If you looked at your system as a series of wires, and if you saw a word attached to each wire, you might find that all these wires, or notes, or messages, are giving conflicting information as to who you are, what you can attain, and which direction you should take.

Some of these messages might be that you are tall, attractive, a good friend, intelligent, a good conversationalist. Other messages might say, "Oh yes, but I feel small in comparison to others; I feel unintelligent; I sometimes find it difficult to communicate; I doubt my own intelligence."

There are other conflicting messages, some of which may have to do with self-worth. You may put yourself down verbally or perhaps allow others to. Your internal computer sometimes goes into overload and cannot cope with the amount of conflicting information that has been fed into it.

Your mind is your most valuable asset. The way you think determines who you are. You need to find a way to look at yourself and to form patterns that are good working patterns for your future. If you drift through life without aim and purpose, usually very little happens. When you apply your mind to what is needed to make your life more complete and workable, you can have amazing results.

The mind is a tool, a functioning tool, and there are more ways than one to get the best from this mind of ours.

Diligent study is the kind where you sit over the books for hours at a time, absorbing the knowledge therein. But there is an adjunct to study that can be even more helpful. If you meditate at least once a day, for approximately twenty minutes, you are moving onto a level different to your normal study level. If you meditated on your studies, you could achieve a higher level of accuracy and intake.

When you have a goal towards which to work, it is good to prepare yourself by sitting quietly for a period of time each day, working on this particular goal.

Because the mind is receptive and attentive, it will use the images that you put into it. If you see yourself studying well and being successful, then surely you will be. If you see yourself failing, then of course that will happen.

Although no one wants to see themselves fail, the feeling of confidence and security is sometimes lacking. Then it is as if the goal diminishes and something less than the ideal must be accepted.

Beliefs and ideas flourish or die according to the importance we have given them in our lives. However, there are certain beliefs that must be incorporated into our system, beliefs about who we are and what we are, how important we are to others and ourselves. If we believe we are unimportant, then we become unimportant. That is our belief. If we believe we have value, then we have, and we need to build up that value inside until it becomes stronger and stronger, until it totally belongs within us.

Developing creativity

If you want to develop your creativity in any way, see yourself doing whatever it is and achieving the result that you want. If your goal is to paint, see the paintbrush in your hand and the picture appearing on the canvas. See the colors changing, being altered; see the landscape in front of you being transferred from nature onto the canvas.

If your creativity is in the form of music, see yourself using the instrument of your choice and hear the music pouring forth. See yourself writing the music and perhaps also performing it.

We can enjoy the creativity of others by going to art galleries, theaters and restaurants, by buying lovely clothes, by looking at the universe and what nature has formed for us.

Creativity comes in many different forms and is not restricted to any one area. It could be painting or drawing, perhaps not in a recognized fashion but in a way that is uniquely your own. Perhaps you see yourself cooking things you like in your own style, writing, dancing, sewing, ice-skating, sculpting, making hats, pottery, writing computer programs. There is no end to your creativity once you can accept that you are creative.

Whichever way your creativity expresses itself, encourage its growth by working with it while you are in the meditative state.

Meditation and study go hand in hand. Meditation enhances the study processes, enabling you to achieve what you want. In a meditative state you can set goals and reach pinnacles that you thought were unattainable.

We all have creative parts of the self that need to be stretched and allowed to come forth, to flourish. Feel the creativity within yourself like lava flowing through your veins, through your system, being tapped and coming forth. Do not say that you are not creative. Rather look to what you enjoy doing and see that in itself as being creative.

Creativity comes in many different forms and each of these forms needs expression. Think of how you can best express your own creativity and allow your own sense of originality to flourish.

I have used the meditative state to bring into my life what I feel I need. Sometimes I require very little. At other times I ask for my larger needs to be met, and invariably they are. This does not mean I have sat back and waited for things to occur. I have actively worked towards attainment of a goal. At the same time I have also worked on the meditative level to visualize the goal, to see it coming to pass, and to bring it through into my life.

Using the meditations in this book

The brain works at different levels of consciousness. These levels are called Beta, Alpha, Theta and Delta. Beta is the normal conscious level, the level at which we work in our daily lives.

When we go into a meditative state we are going into Alpha, the state that enables us to create scenes and images on the screen of our mind. We can attain Theta as we go more deeply into the meditative state. Delta is our sleep level. Most of us work very well within Alpha and come back feeling refreshed and renewed.

It is up to the individual to decide how long to spend in meditation. If you can spare only five or ten minutes, that can be ample. However, to feel the full benefit, twenty minutes is better because meditation can promote calmness, relax tension, and give relief from anxiety as you become detached from your problems. Your problems will not necessarily go away, but meditation can be beneficial to the way you handle those problems. Sometimes the solution comes when you take the time to sit quietly.

The meditations in this book are not just pleasant imagery; they are positive tools to be used in:

1   releasing fears
2   attaining a positive attitude
3   problem-solving

Perhaps some of your attitudes have become negative through lack of direction or difficulty in expressing your innermost feelings and thoughts. You may think things are more difficult than they are, but a new perspective on problems will make them easier to solve.

All the meditations are visually rich and all take place within your personal garden, a garden where nothing can harm you, where there is peace and tranquillity. You feel the warmth of the sun caressing you; you see the flowers and the grass growing. You open yourself to each experience, so different each time you enter the meditative state. Your garden exists within you and is always accessible.

Each meditation is different and should not restrict you in any way. Allow yourself to flow with the meditations, to enter into them, to enjoy them. Bring back each experience as a new experience for you, and allow the peace and tranquillity to flow through your day, every day.

In **The Mountain and the Caves** (p. 77), you find that the higher you climb the freer you become in your thoughts and attitudes. Entering the caves allows you to look at your achievements and also your fears.

The Mirrors (p. 88) enables you to look at a series of mirrors and see yourself as you are, as others perceive you, and how you would like to see yourself.

Approaching exams, driving tests, interviews, can be very stressful with a lot of associated fear. Am I good enough? Will I remember all I have learned? In **Passing Exams** (p. 73), you will find a positive formula that could be helpful in approaching such situations.

I have written what I call **The Star Prelude** (p. 19) to preface the entry into the garden where all my meditations take place. I ask that you see a Star above your head and bring its light down through your body until you are filled with this light as you sit. There is a Worry Tree that is important because it helps you to go into your meditation with a clear mind. It may take a while before you can really use the tree to its fullest advantage, but it works and it works well.

It is also good to open your heart and fill it with love because we all need to learn to love freely and openly without requiring love in return. In other words, unconditional love. When working with young children, I always invite them to feel the wings of an angel wrapped around them. You too could do this, or perhaps imagine there is a wise person or protector with you. No matter how old we are, we need that security. When you come back from the garden, wrap yourself in a golden cloak and send your energy back into the Universe to be used for the highest and best.

As I have said, all my meditations take place in a lovely garden where nothing can harm you. This garden is not an external garden, but one that lives inside each of us. It is a place to enter that is specifically yours. When you close the gate behind you, you have entered the garden and its peaceful state.

With the gate closed behind you, you can choose any of the meditations in this book or draw upon images in your own mind. That is how it has always worked for me. You see one thing and it leads to another; or you could take the theme from one of the meditations and develop it in your own style.

Meditation is very simple. You can begin by sitting quietly either on your own or with a group of people. It is best to sit in an upright chair – if you make the chair too comfortable, you may fall asleep. Try to wear loose clothing for comfort, but if that is not possible, loosen anything that is tight around the waist or neck so that you do not feel these restrictions. It is not wise to cross your arms and legs as this can lead to discomfort.

You might like to have soothing music in the background, or you might prefer silence. Sometimes I like to fix a scene in my head, such as my beautiful garden; at other times my mind is like a blank screen ready to receive whatever images happen to cross it.

Meditating alone

Decide whether you prefer to meditate in the early morning or late evening, or both. Choose a time when you feel you will be free of interruptions. You don't have to meditate for long periods of time. If you are the type of person who goes very deeply and would rather stay in the meditative state but haven't the time, fix a return time firmly in your mind. You *will* return to that time.

Even though you are alone, begin with the **Star Prelude**, taking the light from the Star down through the body. Work on your heart, leaving your worries on the Worry Tree, joining the Wise Person, and then going into one of the meditations. Read the meditation through to fix it in your mind; sit and relax and let your mind ponder the selected meditation, perhaps changing it to suit your personality or how you are feeling at the time. When you come back, please remember to wrap your golden cloak around you and send the energy you have been using back into the Universe for the highest and best.

Group meditation

I have taught meditation for some years. I invite groups to sit
in a circle on straight-backed chairs, relaxing body and mind,
loosening any tight clothing, and if necessary taking off shoes.
Although it is not mandatory, it is a good idea to remove jangly
jewelry and avoid strong perfume. Perfume or aftershave can
interfere with other sitters whose senses are heightened or who
may be allergy-prone.

    I introduce the **Star Prelude** (p.19), and then I take the
group to a place in the meditation where I leave them for a period
of approximately 45–60 minutes, depending upon how settled they
are and how I feel. The length of time is up to the leader – if you
feel half an hour is sufficient, then that is the right length of time for
you and them. When the group is new, it is perhaps best to start
with a shorter time and gradually lengthen it.

    When I bring the group out, I do so from the place in the
meditation where I left them. Take them back along the path to the
gate, close it behind them firmly, and tell them to open their eyes
when they are ready.

    Some people take longer than others to come back. If you feel
some are staying in the meditative state for too long, call them by
name and tell them to return. Sometimes when we go very deeply,
we want to stay there. However, life beckons and goes on, and so we
must come back.

    I wrap each person up in a lovely golden cloak to close them
off from the meditation level. I bring this cloak down over the top of
the head, wrapping it around the body until it comes below the feet.

I also send the energy back into the Universe to be used for the highest and the best.

If you decide to meditate as a group, it is important that you feel comfortable with each other. Sitting with someone who makes you uncomfortable can interfere with your meditation and vice versa. However, I am sure that if you decide to set up a group, you will have with you only those with whom you are compatible.

When sitting in a group, you will find that the group energy can make it easier to meditate and to see things in your relaxed state. Choose a day and time suitable to all and keep to that time schedule. Do not allow other things to take you away from your weekly meditation group. The consistent attendance will bring many benefits to all of you.

There must be one person to lead the meditation. Normally it is best for the same person to lead the group each week, but you could perhaps take turns. Such rotation gives leaders a chance to hone visualization or imaginative skills and to make each meditation entirely their own.

The person who leads the meditation will not be able to meditate as deeply as perhaps they would like. They have to be aware at all times and able to bring the others back at the appropriate time. If the leader drifts off too far, who will bring the group back?

You might think, when you read, that the meditations are not very long. Please remember that when you are speaking to a group, you will do so in a very slow, relaxed voice, pausing to let the scene sink in, so that the group, sitting with eyes closed and focusing inward, can easily visualize and feel the scene. The way the leader uses the voice is very important. It is best to drop the voice by a few tones and speak more and more slowly, with a soothing quality. There is a hypnotic quality about a low and relaxed voice that can help people into the meditative state.

* * *

What I have written, be it the **Star Prelude** or any of the meditations, has been written only as a guide. You may make any of them your own. Perhaps by doing so you will bring to mind details that I have not included.

The Star Prelude

I want you to see above your head a beautiful, beautiful Star that is filled with white light, lovely white light that shimmers and glows. I want you to see this light streaming down towards you until it reaches the very top of your head. And now I want you to bring this pure light down through your head and take it right down your body until it is filled with this glorious white light.

I want you to feel the light going down your arms, right down, until you feel it reaching your hands and going into each and every finger.

Feel that light going down the trunk of your body, down until it reaches your legs, and when you

INNERSPACE

feel it there, take it right down until it comes to your feet and then feel the light going through each toe.

Now that you have brought this glorious light down, you are a beacon of light and have become as a living flame.

Look into your heart and fill your heart with love for all people and for all creatures, great and small. Can you see your heart getting bigger and bigger? It's expanding because you have so much love in your heart for all people, and the animals, and of course for yourself.

Before you enter your garden, I want you to look at the large tree outside. This tree is called the "Worry Tree." I want you to pin on this tree anything that might worry you – perhaps you have problems with work, or maybe you are having difficulties in your personal life. This tree will take any worries at all, no matter how small or how large. This tree accepts anything that you would care to pin or place there.

In front of you there is a Wise Person who has been waiting patiently for you to come, who will always care for and protect you. Can you feel the love emanating from this special person towards you? Or perhaps you have a Guardian Angel who will wrap golden wings of protection around you before taking you into your garden. The Angel's wings are very large and very soft, just like down. Everyone has their own Guardian Angel or Wise Person who takes care of you and protects you always, so you are never alone. It's important to remember this and to know that you have someone who looks after you with love and care.

Take the hand that is extended, open the gate before you and enter your garden, closing the gate firmly behind you. As you do, the colors spring to life, colors like nothing you have seen before. The beauty of the flowers, the colors, the textures and the perfume – breathe them in. The grass is a vivid green and the sky a beautiful blue with white fluffy clouds. It is very peaceful in your garden; it is full of love and harmony.

CREATIVITY

Creativity comes in many different ways and need not be restricted in any form:

- being able to prepare food in inviting ways
- writing computer programs
- using clay to model and cast figures
- painting
- writing
- dancing
- miming
- sewing
- ice-skating
- tuning an engine

The ways are endless. Creative energy flows when we become immersed in what we are doing, and outside distractions do not disturb us.

Look at your unused abilities and adapt the meditations to bring out your creativity. Don't be restricted by what has been written. Be inventive.

Talents and Creativity will stimulate you to bring forth your hidden talents and creative abilities. We need to look at our abilities in ways that will encourage them to surface.

The Painter shows how you can feel the picture you wish to depict forming on the canvas and how to use vibrant colors or to change them as you wish. You may wish to paint the butterflies, the bees, the flowers or the sky – it is always your choice as to how your creativity will flow.

The Violin brings to life music from a beautiful instrument and allows you to feel at one with the music. You may care to substitute another musical instrument, such as a piano, a saxophone, a flute, or perhaps an oboe, and work with that instrument within the same context.

Writing a Book shows that you can tap into other sources for information. The mind is vastly receptive, able to process information and to come up with ideas and thoughts that can be used. The stone block and inscriptions mentioned are only tools for doing so.

The Rainbow of Imagination will tap into the imagination, perhaps through color, allowing your mind to be fertile and open as you take each of the rainbow's colors into your hand, bringing your creativity to the fore.

CREATIVITY

TALENTS AND CREATIVITY

I t has been raining in your garden but the sun has come out and you can feel its warmth touching your skin. The sky looks like blue silk and the white clouds drift near the shining golden ball that hangs in the sky. The silver raindrops glisten on the grass and the nearby bushes and trees. The flowers look as though they have been brushed by a gentle wet hand.

Your pathway is winding in front of you and there are tall trees guarding it, allowing the sunlight to filter through to the bushes and the flowers nearby.

The grass is soft beneath your feet and springs back as though your foot has not left an imprint.

Nothing dies in your garden; everything is replenished.

Because you are creative, you feel at one with nature and you feel the peace that comes from that bonding. Allow yourself to touch the flowers, to feel their texture, their silkiness, to smell their perfume. Look at a leaf and notice how intricately its pattern is etched. If you break it open, it too will emit a perfume so different to those of the flowers.

Your winding pathway is taking you to a part of the garden you have not been to. It is lush and green and has many plants that belong to the rain forest. The trees reach high to the heavens and you can hear the sound of small birds calling to each other, and insects making their way over the fallen leaves.

Amongst all this beauty, you can see a large log table that has many small boxes placed upon it. Some are wooden, some silver, some gold, some amber, and some are made of materials that you do not recognize. They have different shapes and sizes, and some are plain while others are jeweled or carved.

Each box holds a talent, a creativity that you can develop in yourself. Some boxes will show the gifts you are already aware of, while others will show you talents that may still be dormant within. You have many creative talents, but some of them are hidden away, waiting to burst forth, to blossom.

You are going to choose a box, but first, feel within yourself a creative talent you particularly enjoy, one whose growth you want to encourage. See it, feel it, smell it within, and know that this creative part of yourself is about to blossom.

And then choose a box, whether it be wooden or amber, or made of the finest materials. Open it to see how this box will reflect the creativity you are aware of. Because you are aware you have been working on this inner part of yourself for some time, the box will not only reflect what is there for you but show you how to encourage its growth and receptivity. The opened box may show you how to access your musical talent, which could have been dormant, waiting to be touched. You may choose a box that shows a talent you are unaware of, perhaps the ability to be good at a particular sport.

Perhaps you may care to choose a box without first ascertaining what you feel inside, without knowing what your gifts are. This is one of the most wonderful things – your creativity can be limitless.

Perhaps this chosen box will surprise you. It may contain a creative part of the self that you have been unaware of. First hold the box in your hands, feeling its weight and its texture. Now open it and feel the contents being absorbed into your hands, your mind, your body.

There are many boxes that you can choose from and each reflects different talents. There is no need to hold yourself back by choosing only one, unless that is the one that is going to be totally self-absorbing.

Creativity comes in many different forms and each of these forms needs expression. Think of how you can best express your own creativity. Let these boxes be the emblem for that creativity. You will go forth and produce whatever allows your own self-expression to flourish.

Investigate each box, each talent, and know that your creativity knows no bounds, no limitations. Allow yourself to be unique, allow yourself to be individual, allow yourself to be … you …

THE PAINTER

The sky in your garden is a crystalline blue with a tinge of purple, and it is as though a gentle hand has polished it, taking away the clouds and allowing the sun to hang like a huge golden ball in the sky. The sunlight dapples the pathway you follow and butterflies fly ahead of you, taking you deeper into your garden.

The butterflies fly in harmony, creating a moving pattern of color. Some of the butterflies are very large, with brilliant blue wings and small golden markings. Others are a rich velvet brown with many brown shadings on wings tinged and outlined in green.

These colors are so rich and beautiful that you may feel as though you could paint them. Pause a while and take from the mind to the brush what you feel inside and what you see with your eyes.

The flowers are dressed in their prettiest colors. They stand tall and proud, sending their perfume wafting through the leaves of the bushes and into the branches of the trees. As you go down your garden path, feeling the warmth of the earth beneath your feet, you will come to the Grandfather Tree. The Grandfather Tree is the oldest tree in your garden and he has a lot of knowledge and wisdom. His trunk is thick and gnarled and his many branches are heavy with green leaves moving gently in the breeze.

You could settle with your sketchbook by the feet of the Grandfather Tree and sketch what you see in front of you. It might be a gazelle caught in flight as she crosses the clearing; it might be the mountains in the distance; or perhaps it might be the butterflies.

A beehive stands in the clearing opposite you. There are bees flying to and fro, collecting the honey from the colored flowers nearby. Their gold and black bodies hover near the hive before darting off yet again to gather more nectar for their Queen.

When you have sketched all you see, you may want to reproduce, in color, what these images mean to you. Sometimes what you see and what you draw will not be the same. You might want to change or exaggerate some aspects. And sometimes you might want to reproduce the images exactly as seen.

You may want to use water colors or perhaps you may prefer oils. Whatever materials you would like to use are there for you, by the side of the Grandfather Tree. You can set your easel up and transfer your sketches to the easel, board or canvas in front of you, bringing everything to life in brilliant color.

With so many colors to mix, you will be able to find the exact shadings of what you are seeing. Or you may want to make a color seem richer than it really is. You could strengthen your color by perhaps adding purple or red. Perhaps you could experiment by mixing unusual colors together to get hues not commonly seen.

Allow your imagination to help you. Imagination allows our creativity to flow, to flourish. Allow it to roam, to create, to be.

Paint and paint until you feel you are happy with what you are reproducing. The butterflies, the animals, the bees, the grass and the trees, the flowers and the sky, and that brilliant golden sun. Perhaps there are now some clouds drifting by …

THE VIOLIN

The sun's rays are sending down a warm glow as you enter your garden and the trees are waving their arms in welcome. The air is fresh and clean, and the perfume of the flowers surrounds you as they bend their heads in the gentle breeze. There are small wisps of clouds passing overhead, complementing the azure blue of the sky.

The flowers in their many colors stand tall and proud and their perfume wafts towards you and mingles with the smell coming from the lavender bushes. The earth is soft and warm beneath your feet and you feel the peace from your garden surrounding you.

CREATIVITY

Your pathway takes you deeper into your
garden until you come to the Grandfather Tree.
He is the oldest and wisest of the trees within your
garden. His branches are full and heavy and the green
leaves rustle with the slight breeze moving through
them. You always feel as though this tree has
something to offer you, and each time it can be
something different.

Why don't you sit on one of his strong roots
with your back against his trunk? There are many
birds circling above and some of them are descending
to perch on his branches. Look around and you will
see the deer coming closer to you, and also some
white rabbits. Stretch your hand out slowly; you will
find they will come close enough for you to touch
them.

The Grandfather Tree is moving his branches
and one of them seems to be coming nearer as though
to offer you something. Look closely and you will see
a violin resting among the leaves. Stretch out your
hand and see how the twigs loosen their hold and
allow the violin to drop into your hands.

This violin is very old and has not been played
for such a long time. The color of its wood is rich and
full and you can see it has been loved and cared for.
Its strings are strong and at the correct tension and,

as you pull your finger across them, the sound is magical. It is like no sound you have heard before. Take the bow into your hand and put the violin lovingly beneath your chin, and then draw the bow gently across the strings.

Listen to the music in your mind and you will find it travels down to your hands. Listen to the music in your heart and you will find it connecting with the violin. Listen now to the beautiful music pouring forth from this violin presented to you by the Grandfather Tree; feel yourself being transported by the delight it brings, being taken into another world.

You can feel the music coursing through your body, your mind, and your heart. Your entire system flows as one with the beauty of the sounds coming from this instrument. Look around you as you play. The entire garden seems to be listening and moving in time with the notes pouring forth. Your fingers move faster and faster, never hesitating, never doubting, as the music within your soul floods into the air around you, its beauty touching all who listen.

You become aware of even more music waiting to be composed, waiting to be played, and aware that this violin has been longing to be played, longing to be heard.

You may see some of the "little people" coming forward to listen to your playing, delighting in the magical sounds pouring forth. Perhaps they are ready to dance. The gentle nature spirits, who rarely show their faces, are coming to join them.

Whenever you feel the need to play the violin, return to the Grandfather Tree who knows how to keep it safely for your return ...

WRITING
A BOOK

T he peace and tranquillity within your garden lie around you like a cloak, quietening and preparing you. Many animals are approaching and perhaps you may care to stay with them for a time, feeling their peace and contentment. The air is fresh and clean, and the perfume of the flowers surrounds you as they bend their heads in the gentle breeze.

Further along your pathway, you will come to a clearing surrounded by large green trees. The trees seem to be reaching for the sky, their full branches moving softly as birds come to nestle within their foliage.

CREATIVITY

The sun shines gently, sending fingers of light to pierce through the greenery and the flowers, and dapple the large stone block that stands alone in the centre of the clearing.

As you approach this stone block, you will notice writing paper and various colored pens set out on top. You will also see that this stone block bears many inscriptions.

Some tell you how to write; some suggest inspiration; some show how to create within the mind the text you would like to transcribe; some give you outlines for scenarios that can be transformed from words to film.

Position a sheet of paper and take a pen in one hand. Place your other hand on the stone. At first it feels like an inanimate object, as though it has absorbed all the knowledge that there is. But soon the stone seems to breathe and come to life beneath your touch and now ideas spring into your mind.

Your pen flies across the paper as you transpose the ideas from the mind to the white sheet in front of you. And you write on and on, the never-ending supply of ideas and words pouring forth.

You feel the solitude around you as you write though you know you are not alone. Everything

around you lives and breathes and supplies energy
for you to bring forth the creative being within
yourself.

Look at the stone again. Now you find it has
many inscriptions that you had not noticed before. It
is as though the inscriptions, once they have inspired
you, change. You have a never-ending supply of ideas
welling from their source in the stone.

You may want to write a novel – or a play –
or perhaps it is poetry that will pour forth from
the center of your being. Whatever it is, whatever
the creative expression, allow it to flow forth
unblemished and pure from your true self,
from the inner essence of your being.

Trust that what you write is true for you at this
moment and that it brings you joy and happiness.
The creative spirit is happiest when flowing and
bringing delight and color into lives that might
otherwise be drab and colorless …

THE RAINBOW
OF IMAGINATION

T he trees are whispering to each other and the sky is clear. The sun is a huge golden ball sending down a very gentle heat, and its warmth radiates to where you are in your garden. The trees are moving their branches as they welcome the sun's rays. If you listen you can hear them saying, "Come to me, come to me," because they know the sun aids their growth. The air is fresh and clean, the perfume of the flowers full and rich. The primroses and golden daffodils move slightly, their colors blending together in harmony with the other plants growing nearby.

The trees are pointing you towards the oldest tree in your garden, the tree whose branches hang full and heavy, allowing many birds to rest there. Your Grandfather Tree stands serene and full of wisdom. He is always there and is the sentinel within your special garden.

Why don't you rest against his trunk, feeling the strength of his roots which reach deep into the earth below? One of his smaller branches is bending down to brush the leaves gently across your forehead as though in welcome. This branch will continue to stroke the right side of the brain, bringing your imagination to the fore.

This old tree, who has garnered in his depths the wisdom of the ages, also reaches high into the heavens, speaking to the winds and the clouds to summon a rainbow to your feet. The wind and clouds have been busy in other parts of the garden but now they send a light rain whose drops barely touch you, as the rainbow appears.

The rain is falling like a mist, though the sky remains a bright azure blue with the sun's rays still beaming to where you are. The shower of rain is nourishing the earth and revitalising both the earth and you.

And now see at your feet an enormous rainbow reaching from you into the far distance. Its arch is filled with colors rich and deep, colors you have not experienced before. Put your hand forward and feel the energy that flows from each of the colors. Put both hands around the base of the rainbow and feel the strength emanating from it.

Each color holds something special for you. You no longer need to touch the color as the rainbow itself will fall around you, surrounding you with its light and color. Accept this, acknowledge it, and allow the rainbow to bring your imagination to the fore. Feel the many lights streaming through your mind, highlighting the areas of the brain that are in need. These lights will strengthen your imagination, your creativity, and allow you to see the possibilities of these gifts of yours.

Why don't you now work with one color at a time and see what it suggests to you? You may want to begin with the rose color, or perhaps the violet. Whichever color you choose will be the right one for you. Perhaps you can allow the rainbow to transmit the color that you should be working with. Just sit there and experience each and every color in turn, or all at once, allowing your imagination free reign. Do not try to harness the images, do not try to turn them into anything. Allow them to suggest to you what you can do, how you can best use the creativity buried inside yourself, how you can refuse to restrict your gifts ...

FLEXIBILITY AND STRENGTH

Flexibility and strength are important qualities for us all. Unless we learn to be flexible, we will have difficulties in life and with people. Inner strength can be attained by working on the "who" within, by realizing what values you have.

Being Flexible and Forgiving is a meditation to help you become more understanding of other people. You will in turn become more flexible and forgiving of their weaknesses, and also of your own.

Peer Pressure shows how to encourage your inner self to come forward and to be more self-assured and able to withstand pressure from without.

Releasing Problems helps you to deal with the difficult task of letting things go.

BEING FLEXIBILE
AND FORGIVING

The wind is blowing through your garden, bending the trees and the bushes before it, clearing out the debris that lies in its path. The perfume from the many flowers is being spread by the wind to each part of the garden, so that their gentle fragrance enhances each tree, each bush, each blade of grass. Feel the force of the wind. See the strength of the trees that can bend and spring back.

See yourself unwinding, undulating, moving in the wind and with the wind. See your body relaxing, your muscles and sinews softening, your neck flexible and able to turn easily. See your body swaying with the breeze, in harmony, as though to music, and feel this relaxation moving through to the inner self, the self that has been constricted, that needs to emerge, to come forth.

See yourself becoming flexible in all areas of life, not just with the body but with your thoughts, your actions, your speech.

Because you are becoming more flexible, you will find that you are also becoming more forgiving of the faults of others, and also more forgiving of your own.

Faults are only an attempt at expression on the way to learning, and your faults have won you knowledge that you may not otherwise have gathered. Other people have the same way of learning that can sometimes can be very hurtful. Perhaps they feel negative within, or perhaps hurt by circumstances of which you are unaware, as they in turn are unaware of yours.

Now the wind has dropped and the air is calm. See yourself sitting under a rose bush and feel the dew falling gently upon you. As each drop falls, one of your own hurts goes away and you feel yourself becoming more relaxed within.

Allow each drop to fall onto whatever part is in need, and feel yourself becoming more understanding of others, more understanding of the self. Feel your spine as being more fluid, more flexible, as your attitudes and thoughts change. As you forgive those who have hurt you, so too you will find that you have learned from these judgments, and you have also learned to be non-judgmental of others.

Feel the freedom in the air around you, feel yourself becoming free, becoming light, as you let go of the bonds that have restricted you, and know that they need constrict you no more ...

PEER PRESSURE

The air is fresh and clean in your garden. The sun hangs in the sky like a giant golden globe, sending out gentle rays to touch your body and make you feel good. Small traces of clouds make patterns as they move through a sky of a rich dark blue.

Feel the strength rising from the earth beneath your feet, feel it entering through your soles and permeating your entire body, making it glow and feel stronger than ever before.

The strength of the earth and the freshness of the air surrounding your body are making you feel good within, as the old doubts and negativity are being drawn out from your inner being, being dissolved and removed for good.

As this strength pours through your system, you begin to realize that it is not what others think of you, but what you think of yourself that matters. Your inner self is becoming more self-assured.

See yourself being assertive, able to stand up for yourself, sure of your rights.

Other people in your life have their own fears and worries but these need not affect you. Allow their fears to be, to rest with these other people. Concentrate on your own strengths.

Put your arms around a tree and feel the centrifugal force of that tree moving into you, making you feel centered as the life force of the tree comes into contact with your own.

Feel the love you have for the Universe and the love you have for yourself as you are now, and as you will become. As your love strengthens, you will be better able to deal with your peers and the pressures that sometimes come from them.

There is no need to feel any pressure outside of the goals you yourself desire for your life, now and for the future …

RELEASING PROBLEMS

Your garden is especially beautiful as you enter. There are birds of many descriptions that you have not before encountered. These birds are welcoming you and the animals are coming forward to go with you on your inner journey.

You can feel the serenity and the peace of the garden surrounding you, making you feel good. The pathway you follow is taking you higher and higher and the air is becoming fresher and cleaner. You are carrying a bag on your back, a bag that is becoming heavier and heavier. Small rocks on the pathway dislodge and roll aside as your feet take

you ever upward. The animals that have decided
to go with you on your journey are around you.

Your pathway has led you to the top of a
mountain. From here you can see forever. No matter
which way you turn, the view is endless.

Take the bag from your back and look inside to
see what you have been carrying for all this steep
journey. It seems this bag contains problems that
you have had difficulty in releasing.

Take them out, one at a time, and look at them
carefully – and then let them go!

See your problems being released, going into the
ether and being taken away. Stand on the mountain
top and stretch your arms as though to embrace the
heavens, the winds, and the many stars and planets
that surround you. Feel the universal force and
energy that is coming into you as you stretch out
your arms, as you allow your problems to be released,
to dissolve.

Problems are gifts on the way to learning. From
each problem you encounter you learn how to cope,
to give, to share. You learn how to use the mind to
assess what must be done to release or to work
through that particular difficulty.

Problems can be gifts on the way to friendship.
Sometimes problems can be shared and, through that

sharing, a bonding forms with others that may otherwise never have been.

Welcome your problems as puzzles to be solved, obstacles to be overcome, because in that overcoming you will gather more learning and more inner strength to deal with whatever lies ahead.

Perhaps you are concerned about money – put it out into the Universe and know that you will always have enough to meet your needs.

Perhaps you are concerned about your friendships – know that many last and endure, while others get lost with the passing of time. But the memories of those friendships live on, so nothing is ever lost.

See each of your problems turning from a stone into a flower. Then release that flower into the Universe and know that, by changing your understanding, you have learnt how to deal with your problems …

AIMS AND
ABUNDANCE

We all have aims and there is no reason why we should not have abundance in our life as well. If we take it for granted that abundance will come to us, and if we work on it at different levels, there is no reason why it should not be ours.

Aiming High shows how to look at your aims and goals in a positive way and to do just that – aim high.

The Sea of Abundance shows how to work on achieving your aims by tapping into universal energy.

Butterflies shows that if we allow ourselves to be as free as they are, we are limitless.

Aiming High

Your garden is quiet and tranquil and you can smell the freshness of the grass and the perfume from the flowers. The sun is high in the heavens, warming your body, making you feel relaxed and at peace with the world. The blue of the sky is light and delicate and spreading trees cast a protecting shade for the young plants which are struggling to grow. Feel the freshness of the air, breathe it in and feel it cleaning your lungs.

As you go along your pathway, you will come to a big old friendly tree near a winding river. Lean against her trunk and feel her leafy arms around you while you watch the water glistening in the sun. This water is reflecting in its depths the sun's shining rays and the blue of the sky.

When you look high into the sky, where the clouds are drifting past, you may see written what you would like to do with yourself and your life. If it isn't written there, you may perhaps care to see a plane doing skywriting for you. Now is the perfect time for you to assess your aims and ambitions.

Why don't you lie down and watch the words appear as the plane dips and turns through the sky? Your mind can control the plane and the writing. If something appears that you feel you are not suited for at the moment, you could take note of it and put it aside for another day, another year, in the future.

Your future is unlimited. There is no need to hold yourself back from what you feel could be yours. For some people, having aims and ambitions means aiming for the highest point and not accepting anything less. For others it might mean accepting the mid-point.

Put your aims and ambitions into the sky. Write them strongly and keep adding to them. Some goals may seem out of reach at the moment, but this does not mean they will be so for all time.

Some of your earliest aims may come true later in life. This may be because you will have worked through other issues first, issues which had to be tackled for your growth and survival. Sometimes you may change your earlier aims and go in a different direction. That is fine too, as long as it is what you want.

Project yourself and your thoughts into the Universe, knowing there is no reason why you will not be successful. Know that whatever you set your mind to can be accomplished ...

THE SEA OF ABUNDANCE

Your garden is beautiful, with the scent of roses
drifting through the bushes nearby. The sound of
seagulls reaches your ears, making you think of the
sea. In the distance you hear the crash of waves, and
the smell of the salt draws you down towards the
shore. This is the sea of life, the sea of abundance.
The sea is edged with golden sand that glistens as the
sun's light illuminates each grain.

See yourself before the sparkling waters of the
ocean, its waves rolling in to the shore, swirling up
the beach and back, leaving its imprint in the sand as
it returns to the sea.

This sea is the sea of abundance and plenty, the sea that is the source of all life. All you have to do is to tap into its energy and to realise that the sea has energy enough to meet your needs and the needs of all around you.

And as you watch this sea of life rolling in, with abundant waves, perhaps you need to look at why you sometimes find life restrictive. Why do the things you expect, or work for, not come to you in the abundance you expect? If you query the reasons behind your lack, perhaps you might find you have not tapped into the sea of life. If so, you need to ask yourself why you accept restrictions when you can reach into the abundance that is available in the sea of life.

And here is the sea of life. If you are to capture its richness, how would you do it? Would you use a spoon to place the water into a cup? Or a large wooden bowl? Or could you see yourself filling up a swimming pool to ensure you never run short? Think of all the things that contain water and see what you feel would give you enough for your lifetime.

This is the sea of life, the sea of giving, the sea of abundance, and it is there for everyone. No matter how much you take, you cannot take what is due for someone else because there is always enough for each person.

And why would you restrict yourself by placing your water into a bowl or a swimming pool when you could put in a pipeline from this blessed water to yourself, and have an eternal supply.

Allow yourself to have your direct line, knowing that you can take endlessly from this source which is ever-replenishing and will never run dry. Know too that it is your right, and not selfishness, to be connected to the source of plenty …

BUTTERFLIES

The air is fresh against your skin and the dew is still clinging to the flowers and the leaves of the many trees that flourish within your garden. The animals are flexing their muscles and stretching their limbs as they come to greet you. The many birds swoop from the trees' branches in a flood of color to dip and wheel through the air.

As you walk down your garden path, you will notice a cloud of butterflies flitting above the bushes and flowers. They are so pretty, and their colors are glorious. Do look at their wings, they are so fine. It's as though they have been woven by fairy threads, and then dipped into pots of paint that hold all the colors of the rainbow.

Sometimes we too can feel like the butterflies that fly from flower to flower, from honey-pot to honey-pot, on a never-ending quest for life and its beauty.

Why don't you feel what it is like to be a butterfly and to enjoy flight as they do, to enjoy the flowers and their surroundings? The sunlight dapples through the green leaves and filters through to the ground below, lighting the wings of the butterflies so that some look like golden mesh, and others are as blue as the ocean.

In life we can be a butterfly. We can go from situation to situation, enjoying each one, feeling the freshness of not being grounded.

Allow yourself to soar, to have wings, to fly. To have beauty. To be beautiful. Do not restrict yourself by feeling you cannot go from flower to flower, from one part of life to another. Life and opportunities are unlimited.

Butterflies can mean freedom of choice, of expression. You have so many ideas, so many thoughts locked away inside. Allow them to surface, to flow, to fly. And allow them to be beautiful like the butterflies …

ACHIEVEMENT

Achievement means putting time and effort into what you want to accomplish. If you want to succeed in a job interview, you find out all you need about the company prior to the interview so that you can ask intelligent questions of the interviewer. If you want to achieve in any of the artistic fields, you practice for hours each and every day with dedication to your goal. If you want to write computer programs, you learn all there is to make your goal more easily accessible. Whatever you do, have a positive self-image and see yourself being the best *you* there is.

Preparation for Learning shows that no matter what we do in life, we need to be prepared for it.

Learning says to look at your mind and to allow that your mind is uniquely your own, with your own ideas and thoughts.

The Screen allows you to look at your alternatives on a moving screen, changing them as you change your hopes and plans.

The Doors of Choice takes you into a crystal building where things hidden behind each door will be revealed to you, enabling you to make good choices.

Passing Exams shows you how to go into a peaceful state and to examine your knowledge, knowing that you can achieve the required result.

In my book *The Inner Garden* I have written meditations on **School**, **Exams** and **Floating**, which are also aimed at achieving goals. **The Universal Library** in another of my books, *Sunshine*, shows how knowledge is contained in various rooms and you can enter one room at a time to learn all that it holds, before going to another.

PREPARATION FOR LEARNING

Your garden is full of life and color. As you enter you notice that the air is fresh, with a delightful newness. It is as though the dew, which has recently formed on the roses and the daffodils, is sending a special aroma to greet you.

Feel the peace and tranquillity of your garden entering your body, and flowing through your system, bringing an inner sense of wholeness that is new to you.

Allow yourself to breathe in this peace, this wholeness, this tranquillity. Now breathe it back into the garden so that whatever you take in is being returned to its source. By taking the freshness of the garden into yourself, you feel fresher and cleaner than ever before.

See yourself settling down upon the grass, so smooth and green, your back against a stately old oak tree. Overhead, its branches are laden with heavy green leaves, shading you from the golden sun.

The trunk of this old tree supports you and, as you relax against it, you feel its life force entering your body. You can feel your energies, your sense of purpose and your drive becoming stronger. Now you feel also a sense of calmness and serenity. The ground beneath you reminds you of the magnitude of the earth itself and you feel a bonding with the earth, the tree and its roots, which penetrate and grip the earth.

See before you what you need to know to accomplish your ambitions, your aims, your goals. Know that whatever goals you are setting for yourself, you have the ability to achieve.

Look at what you need to learn if you are to accomplish these things and know that you are preparing yourself for what lies ahead of you. Your mind is clear and sharp and yet, filled with the strength of the tree and the earth, you feel relaxed, knowing that you are absorbing everything you need to know.

All doubts and fears crumble and disappear as if they never were.

You feel the sun's glow surrounding you, encouraging your own growth in many ways. You feel good about yourself – how you look at life, how you feel inside. You know that the pathway you have chosen is right for you; that there are many pathways and you need not restrict yourself to one.

Allow yourself to feel the learning that you need pouring through your mind, your body, your heart, so that you are at one with yourself and your future achievements ...

LEARNING

Y our garden is rich in color and the trees bend their
branches to acknowledge your presence. The slight
breeze brings the scent of flowers around you. A
lion is coming towards you, his large mane framing
his head. He is placing his head underneath your
hand before standing with his paws placed on your
shoulders. His roar of welcome resounds throughout
the garden, but then he nuzzles your face to show
you need have no fear.

Now the lion is taking you through the garden
to a waterfall. The sun's rays turn the droplets of
water into gems flying through the air, sometimes
landing where you stand. Perhaps these droplets

ACHIEVEMENT

remind you of ideas that float about, showing how some ideas do not always stay with you but go on to be changed, whilst others remain pure and unblemished.

Your ideas color your life and show how your mind is different to other minds. If you work on your mind, and your ideas, in relation to what you need to learn in life, then surely your life will flow like the waterfall, full and strong, catching the sun's light.

See your mind as being open and receptive to learning, never fearing what is presented to you, nor in what format it comes. See your mind as sharp, clear, active and able to take in what your teachers speak about, no matter which subject.

Subjects you have not been happy to learn become easier as you discipline your mind to accept that you need to apply yourself, to take notes, to ask questions, to discuss, to read, in order to understand. Reading and writing, listening and speaking become easier and more fulfilling as you become familiar with the subject matter and find you enjoy what you are doing.

Never fear what you do not know. It is only fear that will hold you back. Have the courage to question and be curious. Your own abilities will come to the fore and, if you allow it, your mind will be sharp and able to take in all that is being taught.

Put your mind in front of you, look into it and see how clever it is and how it works at many different levels. Allow yourself to go into the cells of the mind to find out what makes you unique, what makes you clever, what makes you special. Consider how you can use all these skills to further increase your capacity to learn.

Open up some of these cells and examine each one closely. You will observe they are connected, yet separate. Your mind functions differently to others; it is uniquely your own. Your own thoughts, your imagination, your gifts, your creativity, flourish within these cells, which need to be nurtured in order to grow.

Learning is a gift in itself and one that is priceless. If the mind is open and receptive, it can take in and deal with concepts and visual images in a way that will surprise you. The ability to learn, and openness of the mind, belongs to us all. Everyone has the capacity to learn, to absorb, and to feel the confidence that flows from knowing your subject, from feeling good about what you are learning, what you are doing.

Treat the mind like a garden that has not only many trees and beautiful flowers but also many animals, birds and wildlife, lakes and rivers. Feed the mind, nourish it, nurture it, and watch it grow ...

THE SCREEN

Y ou can feel the warmth of the sun's rays caressing your body, making you feel good about yourself. Its rays are penetrating to the core of your being, entering your mind as well as your body. In your garden the gentle breeze stirs the heavily laden branches of the many trees that line your pathway, and the smell of the magnolias drifts through the bushes, mingling with that of the rose garden nearby.

Some of the bushes are beginning to flower while others cluster together, their various shades of green complementing each other. There are violets and pansies growing nearby and the deer have come to graze upon the soft grass. You can hear the sound of water and, as you go towards it, you will notice a small opening between the bushes, an opening that makes you want to explore.

Push the bushes aside and you will find you have now entered a part of your garden that seems especially magical, filled with small flowers of all colors and surrounded by large trees. There is a waterfall nearby, sending its spray high into the air, its drops catching the light from the sun, making them appear like colored gems or crystals splashing about.

There is a carved stone seat nearby and, if you choose to sit there, a screen will appear before you showing you many career choices. Feel yourself settling comfortably onto this seat and send out the thought of what you might like to do and it will appear on the screen. When you want to change it, think of another alternative.

Perhaps you want to enter the medical profession. The screen will light up and take you completely through the study processes you would need to accomplish your goal. It will then take you forward to show how you would feel working in the hospital, or even in your own health center. The images can take you further into the future and show you discoveries that will be made, so that some illnesses become obsolete.

Think about being an archaeologist and the screen will show you what is required to enter this profession. It will also take you into various digs around the world, enabling you to discover tombs and cities as yet unfound.

This screen will show you the legal profession with all its learning, and how the solicitors and barristers argue their cases, while the judge makes wise decisions. You may see yourself learning all there is to learn, becoming successful, and perhaps becoming a judge.

You may contemplate being a chef. The screen will pick up your thoughts and show you the best way to accomplish your desire. It will also show you recipes and how to present food in newly imaginative and creative ways.

You may have a love for textiles and color. The screen will show you how to best use this gift with imagination and flair.

Your desire may be to become a train driver, a policeman, a secretary, a miner, a nurse, a writer, an artist, a carer for the aged, a carer for children, a flight attendant, or a pilot. There are so many things you can choose. Investigate as many possibilities as you can. Whatever your desires, the screen will put the images before you, enabling you to see yourself performing, and performing well, the duties of each vocation.

Whenever you wish to see your future work, always come to this magical part of your garden; come and see the benefits of the profession you have in mind.

Project yourself upon the screen and allow the screen itself to show what you are best suited for. You may be surprised at what will eventuate ...

THE DOORS
OF CHOICE

The sun is a rich golden yellow and spreads light
dappling through the trees, its gentle rays falling
around you like a cloak. The sky is a brilliant blue
and reflects the sunlight into all areas of your garden,
enabling you to see everything. Even the shadows
reflect the light, enabling the smaller plants to feel
the warmth of the sun whose gentleness encourages
their growth.

    The trees are standing tall and straight, as
though trying to reach the heavens above, and their
green leaves shine in the sunlight. Some of the bushes
are in flower, whilst beneath others small animals
sleep. The white lilies show their faces, and the

magnolia trees send their beautiful perfume floating through the garden.

Your pathway is taking you through the trees to a beautiful lake. The water gleams in the sunlight, and the many colored fish swim contentedly beneath the water's surface. Ducks and swans gracefully make their way through the water, their sounds filling the air.

Nearby a large building gleams in the sun's light. It nestles amongst the bushes and trees, and is surrounded by flowers of all descriptions and colors. It seems to be made of neither brick nor stone nor glass. It appears to reflect everything nearby and is multi-faceted, like a crystal. Looking at it you may perhaps see several colors as being dominant, but as you move further around its perimeter, other colors take over.

The doorway is open and the entire building seems to be filled with light. Why don't you go inside? Feel yourself going up the stairs to the main entrance. Enter the foyer, and see the various statues and symbols that decorate it. Leading from this foyer are many corridors and each one has many doors.

These are the doors of choice. Go along the corridor you have selected and look at these doors carefully. Each one, although made of crystal and

ACHIEVEMENT

light, looks different. Each one bears an inscription that only you can understand. As you look, you will see one of these inscriptions light up with an intensity that was not apparent before. This is the door you must open. Do not hesitate to go inside.

Each door opens the way to something special for you in your life. Each door offers you choices you need to make. Some may be work-related or to do with study, to be healthy, to have a fulfilling life; perhaps you desire to travel, or you wish to be successful in your chosen field.

Open the first door that has attracted you and go inside. Only you have the key to what you shall find. Only you can retain the knowledge that is in this room and work with it. Only you can have these experiences. You may find a person within each room who has knowledge and expertise in your field. If so, do not hesitate to ask the questions you need answered to find your pathway.

The doors that you are meant to open now will be lit from within, making their inscriptions glow. The doors that may be duller now will glow for you when the time is right.

Do not restrict yourself to one door. Open the doors that are there for you now, knowing that you can return at any time for the others ...

PASSING EXAMS

Y our garden is v-e-r-y quiet; even the trees seem to be standing quietly, not moving a leaf. The green of the trees and the grass is very lush, and the brilliant flowers in their many colors of blue, yellow and purple are scattered throughout, complementing the occasional pink and mauve flowers nearby.

The animals are hushed, with their ears pricked, and the small grey rabbits have paused to listen. Listen carefully, what can you hear? It seems that the Grandfather Tree is moving his branches to acknowledge your presence and would like you to sit at his feet. Sit down and feel the warmth of the earth penetrating your body. Place your back against his

ACHIEVEMENT

thick, firm trunk and feel yourself settling comfortably into the bark as though it has become a cushion supporting your spine.

The Grandfather Tree is aware that this is the day you must take your exams. He is also aware that you need to feel at ease and comfortable within the self to accomplish your given goal, to achieve the results that you desire.

Place your head back against the bark and feel peace settling within your mind. Feel the peace and serenity of this old tree entering your body, helping to align your resolve, your sense of self, your sense of destiny. Your mind will become clearer and clearer, pushing out doubts, fears, and insecurities as you lean against his mighty trunk, knowing that this old tree has lived throughout the ages, overcoming difficulties and gaining wisdom. Be strong like the tree and you too can overcome and grow, never accepting defeat.

Look at the subjects on which you will be examined and take them clearly through your mind, allowing only clarity and brightness to enter. Feel resolve and determination and a certainty that you *shall* succeed, that you *shall* accomplish your desires, that your resolve is such that failure is not possible.

See each of your subjects lined up before you, draw your bow and send a dart into the bull's-eye of each one. Listen to this old tree imparting knowledge and saying there is nothing you cannot do if your resolve is firm.

Now that your inner strength and resolution have been aligned, now that you have acknowledged that you have no fear, that you will succeed, say goodbye to the old tree and go to the place of learning where the exams take place.

See yourself entering the building, feeling good about yourself, knowing within your heart that you have done the uttermost prior to entering in order to achieve the best results possible.

Take your place at the desk, feeling your heart calm, your system clear, and your mind sharp, alert and lucid. Look at the clock on the wall and know that you will have no difficulty in completing your test easily within the allotted time. Look around you and feel your confidence spreading towards others, making them feel confident within themselves as though they too have been with you at the feet of the Grandfather Tree ...

OVERCOMING OBSTACLES

Obstacles always occur at some point in life for all of us. No one is immune. We learn and we grow from overcoming these obstacles. One of the main lessons is to look at our difficulties and to learn how to overcome them. Why are they there? How should I look at them? What can I do?

The Mountain and the Caves enables you to climb higher than ever before, conquering fear. You explore caves within a mountain, each one representing perhaps a fear, an opportunity, or an achievement.

Roar Like a Lion is about becoming powerful, being able to overcome adversity, while **The Elements** shows how to become strong by facing adversity, knowing we can overcome difficulties.

The Mirrors reflects a different you in a series of mirrors, giving a new perspective upon the self.

In my book *The Inner Garden* the meditation **The Tortoise** says to run your own race and to know that everyone gets there in the end. **Father Time** takes you into the past, the present, and the future, so that you can clarify what your needs are. **The Mountain** gives an entirely different perspective on how to overcome obstacles by seeing something large becoming smaller than you.

THE MOUNTAIN
AND THE CAVES

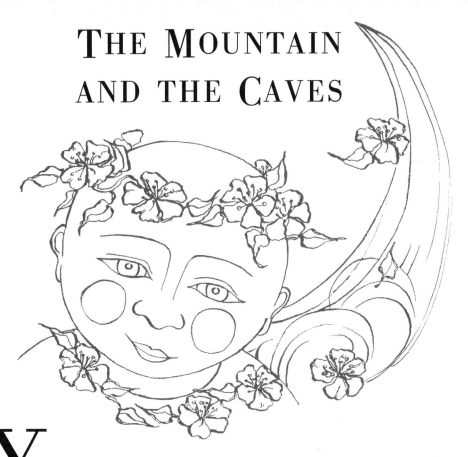

Y ou can feel the peace and harmony in your
garden. The sun is a huge golden ball and the sky
a crystalline blue tinged with purple, with wisps of
clouds drifting by. The grass is soft beneath your
feet and springs upright again as you walk forward.
The flowers stand tall and straight, their vibrant
colors reaching for the sun's light, and the bees are
flying from one flower to another, gathering their
pollen.

The trees are whispering to each other and they
seem to direct you to the mountains in the distance.
The mountains stand serenely etched against the
background of the blue sky, their white tips catching

the small clouds floating nearby. From where you are standing, you can catch a glimpse of a glass building hidden near the top of the mountain. Why don't you investigate?

The base of the mountains does not appear hard to get to. You could either walk or perhaps *wish* yourself there. The mountains stand tall and peaceful, their tops now disappearing into the clouds, which seem denser than before. As you go higher, the pathways are packed with snow and small creatures stick their noses out to see who is walking past. Hardy wildflowers grow within the crevices, surviving in the light from the sun and the moisture from the snow.

You climb easily and steadily upward, your feet finding footholds effortlessly. Your clothing has changed and you notice that temperature changes do not affect you. You feel as comfortable now as you did when you entered your garden.

Look higher above you and you may see small mountain goats moving easily from rock to rock, completely unafraid of the height. You too can move as easily as they, your feet finding the right ledge, the right rock, the right bush to help you along your pathway to the top.

Keep climbing ever upward, knowing that the further you go the freer you become in your thoughts and attitudes.

Higher up you come to caves that you can enter if you wish. In your pocket you will find a small torch so that you see clearly as you enter. Some of these caves may represent your fears, and others your achievements. Because you have had the courage to climb the mountain, you will find that many of your fears have dropped away from you. Perhaps there have been things you wanted to do but fear has restricted you. There is now no need for restrictions, no need for limitations, no need for fear. Go into those caves that hold your fears, face them – and let them go. This will become easier and easier now that you know you have had the courage to climb your personal mountain. Go next into the caves that show your achievements and be proud of what you find there. There are also caves that show you how to accomplish your future desires. Enter them and see what they hold for you.

When you have visited the caves, you may feel like continuing your journey, moving ever upward to that beautiful glass building now hidden in the clouds that wreathe the mountaintop.

Keep going, feeling as though you can leap over the boulders, going from strength to strength, until you come to the crystal doorway. This building represents everything beautiful that you want to achieve or become in your life. Know that you *can* achieve, that you can be anyone you want to be, that nothing is impossible, that all heights are scalable …

ROAR LIKE
A LION

Your garden glistens as you enter and is filled with golden light streaming down from the molten sun, touching the branches and the bushes, nurturing each flower. The sky is an indigo blue and the clouds are small and scattered. The flowers are waving their heads, creating a rainbow of color, as they send their beautiful perfume forth to drift around you.

There are many animals coming forward to greet you and they will follow you as you go deeper into your garden. Put your hand out and touch them – feel their fur, their warm skin, the down on their breasts. Some of these animals may be new to you but you need have no fear from even the largest or fiercest of them. Every creature within your special garden lives together in harmony with every other creature, without fear. The lions and tigers are compatible with the reindeer and the monkeys, while the boldly colored parrots feel as much at ease landing on the animals' backs as on the nearby branches.

One lion comes closer to you than the others. Why don't you place your hand on his neck and allow him to take you further into your garden, into areas you have not been? This lion is very old and wise. He has seen and lived through difficult experiences. He has always managed to survive.

He is taking you into a pit where he fell when hunting and he will show you how he escaped from it. Feel yourself becoming one with the lion, taking on his skin, his fur, his full mane, and you will find yourself pacing backwards and forwards as he did while imprisoned in the depths of this hole. Gather yourself up, feel your huge muscles tensing, and leap towards the topmost rim. Feel the earth sliding beneath you as your paws tip the earth but do not grasp it deeply enough to stay. Fall back into the darkness of the pit. Crouch again and look at the sky and the trees. Look again at the earth edging the top of the pit and then, gathering momentum as you tense your muscles, feel your huge paws thudding against the earth as you leap forward and upward, landing with ease on the ground outside the pit.

Like the lion, you may come across difficulties but you need not accept that your life must be difficult. Like the lion, feel your pride rising to overcome adversity, not accepting the first, or even perhaps the second or third defeat, knowing that you have the ability to succeed and need not accept failure.

The lion is now taking you to a high cliff where he can overlook everything, where there is nothing he cannot see or comprehend. Stand with him to feel the experience of space, of inner strength, of being able to accomplish, of being able to succeed, and roar like a lion. Let your voice out, feel it as being full and strong, feel the power you have within you and, like the lion, let all know that you have succeeded and have no fear ...

THE ELEMENTS

The sky is a deep shade of blue and the golden sun is high in the heavens, warming the earth and all its creatures as you enter your garden. There are small traces of clouds that make patterns as they move through the sky. Look around and you can see the trees and plants all happily sharing the same earth with the flowers and the animals. You become aware of the softness of the air caressing your cheeks, and the warmth of the sun on your body. The branches of the large trees in your garden are bending and moving their branches as they feel the breeze gently ruffling their leaves.

Further ahead birds like sea gulls appear to be circling. Why don't you follow them? The path in front of you is winding through the soft dewy grass, taking you to a hill that isn't difficult to climb. As you near the top, you feel the light breeze sweeping around your body. The breeze becomes stronger with each step. Keep going until you find yourself standing on the crest of the hill, looking down towards a golden beach, where the sand shimmers in the sunlight and the birds make gentle sounds as they murmur to each other.

From where you are standing, you can see for miles in all directions. You can see the sea stretching into the distance and the wide expanse of sand extending along its length. If you look carefully, you may see tiny sand crabs making their busy way through these warm golden grains as the water washes towards the shore. In the distance an occasional ship stands in relief against the skyline, and sometimes a whale can be seen.

Feel the breeze becoming stronger and stronger around you as you go further forward to stand on the edge of the cliff. The once gentle breeze is now blowing full force as though the four winds are gathering to meet where you stand. See the ocean being whipped into white-topped waves as these winds rip across the waters, making the sand fly in all directions.

The wind is buffeting you, trying to dislodge you or make you retreat down the hill. The rain is falling from the clouds that have formed in the sky that was formerly so beautiful and blue, but now turned grey. Feel within yourself the strength to withstand the wind and the elements. Open to them your arms and your heart. Feel yourself becoming one with the Universe, one with the winds, one with the sea, one with the clouds, one with the rain. Feel yourself gaining strength and momentum, gaining self-control, knowing you can succeed, you can overcome, knowing that nothing can hold you back from what you desire to accomplish. Feel your desire to succeed and feel it as a fire within the soul.

Send a call out into the Universe, one that echoes out for all to hear, proclaiming that you are invincible, indomitable, not able to be put down, that your abilities will hold you in good stead throughout your lifetime.

And now you can see the sun is breaking through the clouds and the sky is becoming, yet again, a beautiful blue, but now washed and cleaned. The seas have calmed; the sea gulls are diving over these serene waters; and the sand crabs are again going about their business upon the golden sand.

All the elements have come into play and you have joined with their energy and force and brought them under control. You have the inner strength to know what you want to accomplish, what you need to achieve, and you *shall* allow yourself to do so ...

THE MIRRORS

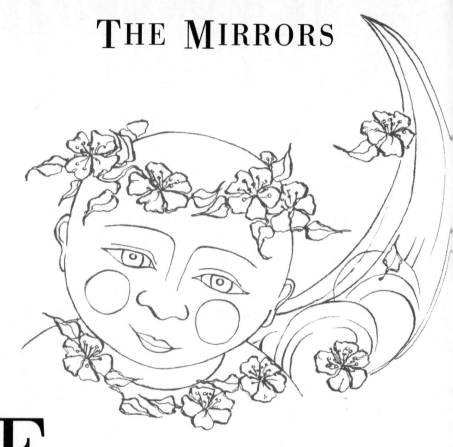

F eel the freshness of the air surrounding you,
caressing your skin and stirring your hair as though
gentle fingers are moving it. The tall trees are
bending slightly in the breeze that ruffles their
branches, and the perfume from the roses drifts
around you. The green grass beneath your feet feels
like velvet and the snapdragons in all their bright
colors stand in relief against the green of the bushes.

Your pathway is taking you deep within your
garden, and you can feel its peace and serenity
coming forward as though to greet you. Experience
yourself absorbing it, taking it in and feeling good
within the self. The very air you breathe is cleansing

the inner person, and will clean out your system, making you feel vital, alive, and full of well-being.

Can you hear the sound of water falling? Follow the sound and you will come to a small waterfall whose drops are being thrown high into the air, so that the light catches them and makes them appear like small gems, before they fall to earth. In the glen nearby, their beautiful fine wings shining in the gentle sun, are exquisite fairies dancing to the music of violins. The fairies are beckoning as they have something special to show you, something that is just for you.

Nearby you see a small rock shaped like a comfortable seat. They would like you to sit there while they place a series of mirrors in front of you. Each mirror has a heavy silver surround with an intricate pattern. Several fairies are setting them up so that you can see yourself from all angles.

Look into the one immediately in front of you. I wonder what you will see? You can see your physical appearance of course, the shape of your head, the slant of your shoulders, and the wisps of hair straying in the breeze.

Look deeper and deeper into the mirror and you will see a depth to yourself that you have not noticed before. Feel as though you are entering the mirror, entering the self. The images you see are reflecting the changing essence of who you are. Perhaps you see a person revealed as being able and complete for others, or perhaps you see the "you" no one else can see, the one that hides inside. Why don't you reflect into the mirror what you want to be? Sometimes it can be difficult to see ourselves as we really are because we may be colored by other people's perceptions.

Why don't you look, now, into the mirrors placed at an angle to see another self?

Stay by the waterfall, sitting on your rock, feeling the sun's warmth on your body. Notice that the sun is not only warming the outer body but also penetrating the inner being, which needs light and warmth.

The mirrors will enable you to see deep inside yourself, to reach areas you have not reached before. As you sit there, you can feel the changes starting within, changes that are necessary if you are to feel more complete, more sure, more able. This mirror will reflect back to you an image not only of who you are now, but who and what you can be ...

PERSPECTIVE

These meditations look at how to accomplish what you need in your life and how to tap into a different way of approaching your needs.

The Pathway to Success allows you to look at both the negative and positive pathways and to work with both.

Clear Sight and Clarity of Purpose enables you to look at your goals and purpose in life with a different focus.

Setting Goals says to look at your goals, to line them up, to achieve them.

Universal Wisdom says that the Universe will supply, and it is there for you to tap into.

Your Belief System is so important – how you feel about yourself, your inner strengths and how, sometimes, your belief system changes.

THE PATHWAY
TO SUCCESS

Feel the freshness of the air surrounding you, the light breeze gently ruffling your hair and touching your skin. The sun is bright, sending its rays beaming down to where you are so that you can feel not only its warmth, but its strength.

As you walk along the pathway through your garden, you will find that the main path divides into two, giving you a choice of directions to investigate.

The sun falls strongly on one pathway, while the other appears dimly lit. Perhaps you should experience this latter one first, for a short time only, because this is the path of negativity.

The negative pathway is the path that does not accomplish what you want in life. You may sometimes be tempted to go down this pathway because it may appear to be the easier one to follow. Perhaps, at certain times, you need to go along this pathway to make your own assessment of what it holds. You may also find that fear can send you along this route – fear of being unable to achieve, unable to succeed, unable to feel good about the self that lives within.

The positive pathway, lit by the sun, allows you to bring the negative into line. The positive pathway shows what you can achieve, despite your fears of the self and of failure to accomplish. Allow yourself to feel free, free to follow the sunlit path, free to feel as though you want to dance, to turn, to leap.

See the two halves of the self meeting as though for the first time and see the brightness entering the shadowed and negative half as though to warm it, to welcome it, to bring positivity to it. Bring the lonely part, the shy part, the misunderstood part, up into the light of the sun and feel the sun's warmth encouraging, blessing you, loving you. And feel the positive part of the self glowing in this light as it overwhelms the negativity that has surrendered.

You can now feel the two halves of the self coming together, working in full cooperation, as though they are one. Your strengths and your weaknesses now work together, in harmony, in love …

CLEAR SIGHT AND CLARITY OF PURPOSE

T he air feels crisp and clean as you enter your garden, and the sky above is a delicate blue. The clouds are small and wispy, trailing across the heavens as though wanting to form patterns they haven't made before.

Your Grandfather Tree beckons you to approach because he has a gift for you. As you stand before him, one of his branches bends down to hand you a pair of glasses, the like of which you have never seen before. These are the glasses of clear sight and clarity.

Open your eyes wide and focus on the future, on your destiny. Stand in the center of the clearing not far from the Grandfather Tree and feel yourself turning around and around. As you turn, everything changes with you. When you face one way, you see the mountains in the distance; another way and you see the seashore; another and you see cities; and in another you see country scenes. And in between these sightings, there are others not as clearly defined.

Perhaps you see something between the mountains, or around them, that you did not notice before. Put your special glasses on, these glasses that enable you to see more clearly than ever before. You will find that you are now able to focus on small details that you could not previously see. There, you can now see a small river running close to the bottom of the mountain with the sweep of the trees on the ridge higher up.

Keep turning and using these glasses to keep your sight clear. You will find there is so much that you have not seen or been able to absorb before.

Move back to the Grandfather Tree and settle down with your back supported by the old trunk. Now you can use these glasses to go inward, to focus on what is important to you. You will find many issues that have been cloudy are now becoming clearer and clearer as you change your focus. You are finding there are more ways of looking within than you realized before and your inner sight is also becoming clearer and clearer.

Your goals and your purpose in life are coming more to the forefront than they were. Some of them are standing in front of you, wanting to be recognized. You have accepted them on the unconscious level, which is how they have arisen in your meditative state; allow yourself now to consciously accept them.

Your inner vision and clarity are becoming as one, your purpose and drive in life are becoming more apparent, and you are feeling an inner strength growing that will help you achieve. You are clear-sighted and have attained the clarity of purpose that you have been searching for ...

SETTING GOALS

Y ou feel a strength and a purpose within the self as you enter your garden. Wisps of clouds are floating in the vivid blue sky and the sun is dominant with its strong rays focusing towards where you are. Shafts of sunlight fall through the trees and the birds are nesting on their branches.

Stand there awhile and allow the warmth of the sun to enter your body, enlivening your spirit, touching the mind, allowing you to look forward to what you want to do for your future. Feel the self within expanding, and accepting that anything you want is possible if you will set your goals, and seeing yourself achieving them.

PERSPECTIVE

The goals and aims and ambitions that you now have need to be brought within striking distance so that you have every opportunity to achieve them. Perhaps you have some goals that must be long-term, and they will be placed further off, but your aim is to accomplish, to achieve, and there is no reason why you cannot.

Line up all the goals you have set, and plan to set, and see yourself achieving them. See yourself aiming for them one at a time. Take aim with a bow and arrow, and see and hear that arrow whistling through the air before striking its target dead center.

Everything is possible for you if you allow it to be so. You set your target, and you also put the name of your goal, or what you want to achieve, on the tip of the arrow, and you send it off, knowing that arrow and target will come together.

There is so much ahead of you, and your range and viewpoint are important. Look ahead to what you want from life and how best to achieve it. See yourself in a few years' time, having succeeded in what you have set and planned for yourself.

Feel yourself expanding as you set your goals, knowing that you do not need to limit yourself. Your possibilities are limitless …

Universal
Wisdom

There are small wisps of cloud floating in the azure blue sky and the sun's rays beam strongly down to where you stand in your garden. The many animals that live in your garden are lying down, basking in the sunlight, loving its warmth on their fur. The smell of gardenias drifts through the air, blending with the perfume from the other flowers. There are brightly colored parrots on the branches of the trees, and the nightingale sings a beautiful song that echoes throughout your garden.

You feel peace and serenity as you wander along the pathway in front of you. The grass is cool underneath your feet, and fallen leaves create a carpet for you to walk on.

You have a sense of the Universe never changing, being whole, being there to tap into. Perhaps you have needs that are not being fulfilled. If you connect into the universal energy, you will find that the Universe will supply fulfillment.

There are many ways of attracting this universal energy and each of us must find the way, or the image, that suits us best.

You may see the Universe as a giant computer where, by tapping into the correct program, understanding of how the Universe works will flow for you. If so, you could see before you a huge screen showing what is there within the Universe and its environs. Push the red button, sit back on the chair in front of the screen and see what comes up on the screen.

You may see the Universe as other worlds, other stars, other planets, all connecting to ours, with their own knowledge and wisdom.

You may see the Universe as our world rotating within other worlds, with knowledge and ideas flowing around it, waiting for the right person to take this knowledge, these ideas, and make them work.

Universal knowledge and universal ideas are
there for all. The Universe will provide; feel as one
with the Universe.

Connect with the higher power, the higher
energy, and see how it can work for you. See which of
your ideas are not being fulfilled – perhaps you want
to write a book, achieve your aims, change the self –
and put these ideas out into the Universe, connect
them up. Now see how you can bring these dreams,
these thoughts, these wishes into fulfillment …

Your
Belief System

In front of you is the most beautiful tree you have ever seen. It is tall and straight and its branches are full, with bright green leaves shining in the light that comes from the luminous sun overhead.

Each branch represents an area of your life and your beliefs. Each leaf on this branch represents how you have worked on changing your beliefs. You may find as you look at this tree, its branches, its leaves, that some of the green leaves either have turned brown and started to fall or have already grown old and stale and fallen to the base of the tree, to replenish the earth and the roots of the tree.

Feel yourself growing as the tree grows, feel the strength that comes with having secure roots that are constantly being nourished. Nothing is ever lost. Every idea you have ever had, whether used or discarded, has led to where you are today, and who you are. Ideas flow like the tide. Some are left on the shore and others go back into the sea to be replenished and to come back stronger than ever.

One branch represents how you feel about your own inner strengths. Another represents your value system. And there are others that deal with your kindnesses, your thoughts, your feelings for others.

The tree represents yourself, with a firm trunk and a firm idea of who you are, with your roots going deeper and deeper into the earth as you grow ever upward, reaching for the heavens and the light that acknowledges your growth.

Feel your strength and know that each new leaf that appears shows your learning, each sturdy branch your knowledge and your expertise.

Belief systems change with the years and you will find that some of the beliefs you have grown up with no longer apply. Therefore you will change them, because *you* need to change. We accept other people's ideas and viewpoints as our own until we

PERSPECTIVE

103

discover we have the ability to enjoy our own ideas and viewpoints and beliefs.

Allow your belief system to be open, to be flexible, to be free ...